REVERSE WORLD COLORING BOOK

BY INES J. SARAN

CHRISTMAS

BOOK TEN

Unleash your creativity and imagination

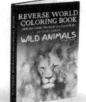

Use this QR code to easily locate our books.

Dear Friends,

Thank you for exploring the world of reverse coloring with my book! If this creative adventure has brought you joy, I would be incredibly grateful if you could share your experience through an Amazon review.

Your insights have the power to brighten someone else's artistic journey and also fuel my enthusiasm to continue creating for you!

I genuinely appreciate your role in spreading the creative and calming vibes of the Reverse World Coloring Book.

Can't wait for our next creative adventure together!

Brighten Amazon with your glowing star review! Snap the QR code and let your words sparkle.

thank♡you

Discover the Magic of the Reverse World Coloring Book!

Reverse coloring is your ticket to a world **of imagination and creativity!** Imagine you have a canvas filled with colors, but the story is yet to be told. It's your task to create the tale by **drawing lines, shapes,** and **playful doodles** that bring the picture to life!

But wait, there's a bonus! This book isn't just about colors and lines; it's your **escape** into **inspiration, your oasis of relaxation,** and your shortcut to a more **serene mind.** As you flip through these pages, picture **tranquility** seeping in, **harmony** settling around you, and **mental clarity** sharpening like never before. Ready to dive in and make these pages your own? **It's time to let your creativity shine!**

To help you embark on your artistic journey, here are a few helpful tips:
1. Your **choice of pen** or marker is key; it shapes your artwork. My personal preference leans towards Pigment Liners with a 0.5 - 0.8 mm fine tip or playful Gel markers.
2. If you use thicker markers to **prevent bleeding** to another side, please use a blank page in between.
3. **Fearlessly experiment!** There are no right or wrong choices when it comes to reverse coloring.
4. Most importantly, **enjoy yourself!** Reverse coloring is a fantastic method to ease stress and let your creative energy flow freely.

Join the community of creatives from all around the world and showcase your unique artistic style. Once your masterpiece is complete, don't forget to share it on social media using the hashtag **#ReverseWorldColoringBook** and tagging **@ReverseWorldColoringBook** to **unlock how-to videos, special freebies, and giveaways.**

This book proudly takes its place as the **tenth edition** in our esteemed **Reverse World Coloring Book series.** For more ways to ignite your creativity, explore our various themes: **Baby Animals - Kids Edition, Flowers, Cat and Women, Mandalas, Dogs, Plants, Sea Life, Wild Animals, and Abstract.** Alternatively, simply type "**Reverse World Coloring Book**" into the **Amazon search bar.**

I'm excited to see the beautiful artwork you'll create, making this a cherished gift for anyone seeking moments of calm and creativity during the holidays.

Connect with me on Instagram, YouTube & TikTok
@ReverseWorldColoringBook #ReverseWorldColoringBook
www.ReverseWorldColoringBook.com
ines@ReverseWorldColoringBook.com

Merry Christmas
BEST WISHES
And a Very
Happy
New Year

Ines J. Saran

Reverse Coloring ideas

Are you ready for **some inspiration?** Let these drawing ideas **spark your imagination** and lead your artistic adventure.

Instagram, Tik Tok and YouTube @ReverseWorldColoringBook

For an extra **burst of creativity, scan the QR code** and dive into a fantastic **Reverse World Coloring Video.** These resources will make your doodling and drawing adventure even more exciting and fun!

love

<u>Friendly tip:</u>
Slide in a blank page to
avoid bleeding through,
especially while using
thicker markers.
Enjoy your reverse
colorful journey!

HAPPY HOLiDAyS

Thank you for exploring the world of reverse coloring with my book! If this creative adventure has brought you joy, I would be **incredibly grateful if you could share your experience through an Amazon review.** Your insights have the power to brighten someone else's artistic journey and also fuel my enthusiasm to continue creating for you! I genuinely appreciate your role in **spreading the creative and calming vibes** of the **Reverse World Coloring Book.**

thank you

Made in the USA
Las Vegas, NV
24 November 2023